Making Faces

Making Faces

K. A. Wisniewski

HOT AIR PRESS
CHAPBOOK SERIES / 2016

Hot Air Press is a collective of artists, designers, and writers in the Mid-Atlantic dedicated to the creation, support, and sponsorship of public art projects and regional artists and writers. Our studios are located in Philadelphia, Wilmington, Baltimore, and Charles Town.

First published in 2016 by Hot Air Press, Baltimore, MD.

Cover concept by K. A. Wisniewski.
Graphic design and typeset by Bill Rutherford.
Printed in the United States.
Copyright © 2016 K. A. Wisniewski.
All rights reserved.

ISBN-10: 0-692-72205-X
ISBN-13: 978-0-692-72205-3

Cataloging-in-Publication Data is available at the Library of Congress.

Library of Congress Control Number: 2016908531

❋ "Why do you make such faces?"
~Shakespeare, *Macbeth*

for Molly

Table of Contents

How to Fold a Map

Who still needs a map?
Driving up to see you
doesn't mean moving north.

Nobody reads legends
or takes the time to decode
the map's corner keys,

the analog compass
on our screen switched off
with the flip of a button.

The old road maps paint a better picture.
Various sides tucked away inside each other—
Flat, creased, balled-up.

We might brag about where we've been
or dream (or dread) where we're going—
argue about the meaning of signs.

We all know the shape of the earth.
Round, like a ball. One-sided figure—
So aren't we on the same surface?

We'll follow the shoreline
until there are no more roads.
Two people with a map, still lost.

Hands Off

They aren't friends, just big kids who like to see the show, like
to see the drama, the explosions, someone else's hurt feelings

spread across the lawn. It was worth the anticipation:
the idea of the blast, the noise. M-80s, cherry bombs, breaking out

of themselves. A couple of pumps of the air rifle. I asked them to shoot
me with my own bb gun, hoping we'd be friends.

And there was the rush of breaking in, hopping fences, stealing
sulfur and nitrate from Mr. Tom's shed and charcoal

from my dad's back porch. Filling up a shampoo bottle.
Blowing up a letterbox. Lighter fluid burns quicker.

I kept reminding myself I could light my new coat
on fire and roll down the hill and watch everyone applaud.

I was floating alcohol on the water, scarred and bruised with hands
that never worked the same again. But that summer I had friends.

Harvest Mice

We are harvest mice,
nestled, settled, tightly curled,
but our hearts are louder than bombs.
Wierna rzeka: It played music
like noise, Papa says,
before the noise of bombs became music.

Papa remembers saving
wrappers of butter and peeling labels
from jars, complains that the rye bread
doesn't taste the way it did.
I remember the berries
that stained Babcia's dress.

I saw the rubble, I heard the bombs, I felt my chest.
He knows the grass, he smells the river, hears tears.

Papa says,
the Poles are last
of the dreamers.

Grandfather Tongue

You were an unknown world,
traces I saw engraved
in the lines and angles
of my grandfather's face,
a mouth that puckered around
the stem of a pipe filled
with Tip-Top tobacco
and that came into focus
through a drifting cloud of smoke.
I leaned in, listened to
the strangest of words,
hybrid of nonsense phrases
that meant nothing at all
and yet made a sense between us:
those tentative and ephemeral sounds
inadequate to any form of memory.

Tova

Catholic is universal, but
love has its limits. We could listen
to jazz—those old records bought
together from the Soundgarden
in the old neighborhood—waltz
in the living room, brave the morning
sun. I could pull the hair out of
your mouth during dinner and you
could show me where you want me,
and I would bend. We could both
seek reconciliation. But in one family dinner,
the tongue sweeps back inside.
"Those Goddamn Jews!"
You are the brunt of every joke. I sit there
watching you take it. Chewing,
swallowing, (and trying not to look)
around the table, at the empty space
between us left empty.
What kind of name is Tova anyway?
They ask the first anniversary you are gone.

Cold Coffee

It is in Krakow where
she tells me that cold
coffee makes me beautiful.

I dip my finger in the red
river of berry juice traveling
around my saucer as

my eyes rise, reflecting
the pregnant swelling on
the table. It is summer.

We watch one another's
watchfulness, the celestial
face brushing our brows,

the heated look that harvests
long kisses like cloudberries.
She sipped the sap on my

finger, cleaned the puce
pulp stains with her tongue.
It lasted all afternoon.

A blue shadow fell upon us
in the shape of an apple. I sipped
cold coffee, felt beautiful.

Shopping in Tuscany

Our Tuscan sky titters
an insolent golden haze
in autumn, drapes birdsong
shadows into the streets
and alleyways as you shop
for a Sunday dress and I trail,
listening to your heeled-boots
strike a steady rhythm.
Ballerina rows of birds
dip and lift and curtsy.
They play in puddles,
bicker over bread.
One colored burglar steals
a pastry from a little girl.
My pocket wishes for space
to take the little dodger home
as your feather-tipped finger,
delicate and demanding,
points into my chest
before it slips folded notes
from the inside sleeve.
Old men playing cards at a table
across the street can only laugh.

Camera Obscura

The street was narrow,
wrapped like a blanket
around the city.
The wind curled itself dry
in the square,
and the buildings were disaligned
like a little girl's braid.
I didn't notice Marissa's body,
a runestone smooth from wear.
We were both bored,
having already seen everything
photographed and cataloged
in books loaned from the library.
And in the lieux de memoire,
we were both liars,
already planning the stories
we would tell when we returned home,
writing fairy tales on postcards
to mom and dad, her sisters
in Sarasota and Pittsburgh.
There was never a moment
we didn't look at each other
through a wiped lens.

In Dresden at Dawn

Giant of shadow and light and sweat,
Vermeer glows like from another era
on the walls of a Dresden museum
that looks like a cathedral. He is
misunderstood here, out of place
next to deep Hungarian blues
that could come to life and drown
the yellow lady, the green apples,
the muted instruments, and ruin the letter
that might not ever be read again.

Rachael's Story

It was the most intimate way
we'd ever touched: his belly
reddened by smearing sap from trees
I grazed on our hike with my parents'
little dog in tow.
The curved autumn moon,
already visible in the afternoon,
made him feel self-conscious.
He was cold, hard,
ready to return to the car.
I stopped and told him
I felt like a giraffe, tall and awkward
and all alone. His eyes never strayed,
even when I rubbed the syrup hard
into his course, black hair, searching.
He wanted to kiss me, but he never did.
When I hear his name,
I still feel stickiness on my hands.

Japonica

When Loretta took down her braid,
her hair fell just below her exposed
shoulders, the color of a bottle
of Spanish Rosado. She sucked in
the Hookah, pressed her mouth onto mine
and blew out, an exchange of heat.
I pointed through the window at the brilliant
white blossoms of a japonica in the garden.
She named it, exposed its mystery:
"They shouldn't get to be that big."
I exhaled. There was nothing left in the Hookah.

Venus and Mars, the Leviathan

Darkness falls at the beginning of June
and Venus and Mars align
for the first time in eighteen months.
Mars marches up the stairs like a leviathan,
punches the wall and shouts, "I love you."

A beehive star cluster stops and stares with drinks
and napkins of niblets in hand.
Frozen in space, they merely watch
the planets rotate round the porch through
a window that conceals all reddish tint.

The surface of Venus is suddenly exposed.
Sulfuric fears are clear by tears.
Gravity is steadied when Mars maintains,
"I'll never leave your side again."
Even though Venus knows this

alignment only happens once in eighteen
months, she takes him in, an embrace.
One guest puzzles at his window view.
Another guest pulls him away, whispering,
"There is nothing to be learned by staring."

Rendezvous

Anything with a silent z—
a word for lovers and spies
and flying machines that promise
to take us to another time.

What else could substitute?

Cheap fans—glorified straws
that spin in the wind
like futuristic flowers
propelling us to a youthful ecstasy.

In the middle of rendezvous
there is a silent *z*.

Move-in Ready Monday

On move-in Monday, clothes in the corridor, we chase each other,
like warriors, racing to the top of the stairs of a ruined castle.

You are the Queen of Scots
reborn, red-haired and black-skinned.
Your royal blue robe flaps in the spring winds,
smacks me on the face and provokes
a cigarette-smoked battle.

You pull on an imaginary bow
and release, hiding between pillars
after each shot. You grip rock, looking wide-eyed
at me, taking shots of you on my Canon.
My dry, detailed, pedantic speech
on dungeon skeletons
brings gravity.

I advance and you retreat to arms.

If I am the master sentenced to starve to death, you are the bitch
tied to the tree. Here, there is no bravery, no loyalty, no beer.

Studio

We are several years too late
for sharing the space of a studio,
one crammed room with nothing
except a kitchenette and a bath.

Designated places is uncharted
territory: the toilet for reading,
and, above the fridge, a tiny TV.
The bed is for love and sleep.

Only our striped kitten roams free,
a migrant gypsy we claim to be.
One night one room is too much;
others, no distance is great enough.

We learn: I'm not a man to be
disturbed, and you're not a woman
to cry over such mundane things
as burnt buns and overcooked pasta.

Tonight, we might spend hours in separate rooms,
but we don't. We negotiate space into a familiar map.

Stalagmite

At 9am, a call confirms nothing
will ever grow in your belly.

It comes as we wait in a lobby
modeled like a locomotive terminal.

In the gift shop, we buy
cheap hoodies and drink

warm cups of coffee in Styrofoam.
Children scream and laugh

in the distance, echoing in the open
hall as the adjacent elevator door squeals

open. We are still silent, next in line
with a family of five, a herd

from Oklahoma with one pouting teen
and a crying babe—a little tike

still attached to his mommy's
tummy. The middle kid runs free.

Out of elevator, he immediately leads,
interrupting the tour guide's talk at every stop,

while pointing at the ghostly silhouettes
painted on the artificially lit cavern walls.

He shrieks like a baboon at bats
sound asleep in hidden crevices.

He sings into the black and burps
between the silent space between us.

And over railings he reaches rock,
rock that will never grow again.

The Wolves Among Us

There is no beauty to inflections,
no subtlety in my bedtime stories
that try to put my boys to sleep.
Wolves are warnings of monsters

that would eat us the very moment
we close our eyes to dream.
There is no sweetness in finding
children and gingerbread women

who try to beguile with candy castles.
You laugh at the tale of the wolves
downstairs talking to mommy, drinking
Miller Lites and motor oil and budget

reports. The world is a crazy place.
So let us hide under covers together.
Between your giggles, I can hear long
howls and hide in one corner as you settle.

Making Warm Cider

The old view of yesteryear flashes crystal clear as Bella
stirs more cinnamon into the heating pot of warm cider.

Memories are a squirming nest of mice. They scurry in the
crawl space of the attic, under the floorboards, undetected

until some smell, some sound or taste, or, today, the scraping
of a wooden spoon stirs them into a frenzy. It is a recipe for

trouble. A dad stands back, staring at his little girl, barefoot
on a stool, leaning down on the counter and fingering the hem

of her soft, floating skirt. Daughter is transformed into a girl
maybe ten years older, the first one dad told, "I love you,"

the one who taught him how to make cider when they shared
that apartment on Charles, in the tiny kitchen where she

twirled again and again and again, where they made love
until the planets shifted, until the continents unworked their

knot. One love has the face of another one. He watches her
finger down the cookbook, grab the container of cloves. Three

taps of it fall into the mixture bubbling below. A slow breath
as she turns and smiles. Maybe this is why he loves his daughter

so much. She pushes her dark brown tresses behind her ears
before she leaps from her perch with the movement of a feline

animal. The dad draws her in, pulls her hair of womanhood,
strand by strand. The nest of squirming mice is a soft squirming fear.

Mushroom Hunting

Morning shows no sympathy.
But you, sweet old bird lady,
can make light of everything.
When I tell you I've spent all evening
drifting towards a young lobster girl
dangling bait into a trap,
you flutter to my pillow and unfurl
cape-like wings over my shoulders.
Your explanation is soothing.

We all hear the call sometimes.
Strangeness is a welcome guest.

So you ask to feed me garden greens
and fresh pasta with sweet song.
Although some may be toxic,
you ask for a walk along the skinny
river into shadowy wood
for mushrooms, for rekindled love.
Neither of us have done this before,
and neither of us really knows
what we are looking for.

Digging

We were singing
happy birthday,
don't die chants
to our best friend
when the lights
came back on
and you turned
to see me smiling,
still singing aloud,
fingers halfway
up my crooked nose.

The Hermit

lives in a shell
that echoes his past
until he can no longer hear it,
until memory is a cloak two-sizes too small.

The hermit excites
at his brainstorming prowess
at the habit-forming ways he avoids toilet seats
in fear that he'll grow too close to those who sat before him.

Solitaire is the only game he knows and plays
for it's not the size of the shell that wins.
When another hermit enters,
new games are learned.

The hermits share shells, sliding in like a kiss
until they have nowhere else to go.
They would rather die
in the night

knowing that they were
once hermits.

For the Crows

Some dying birds
seek solitude.
They flee
from a secret branch,
hiding from the world's gaze.
But in its closing hours,
the crow is cocked
in full view.
It finds company,
perches for its last days,
stiff and erect,
cawing crowy things.
The crow preens and pecks,
protecting its nest
in the babul.
It values eastern winds
and the rotting flesh
left by the roadside,
and it welcomes
the sycophants
who praise old bones
and the salts of memory.
Their joints gall
at most other things foreign.

Postcard from Lisbon: The Fisherwives

Off the commercial
crooked streets
of Lisbon
and its thrifty
lights of life,
a low hum
of busy beings
toil away.
As sails are sewn
and motors disabled,
drifting vessels dock.
Whiffs of fish and fresh
garlic belch up the alleyways,
those serpentine-shaped alleyways,
giving garlic glimpses of
weather-beaten wives
lifting loads of line and legers,
dragging the oceanic plunders
down the wooden planks.
The fisherwives of Lisbon
are mermaids shaken
from similar nets
and dropped on dry land.
The port transforms
into a warehouse of wharf-talk.
But the shore-bound sirens persist,
dragging, cutting, icing . . .
wearing seashell necklaces, fish
basket bonnets, swishing
scale-covered skirts
that slog like slimy
glittering tails,
trailing wisps of sea-weed
back to their earthen homes.

Acknowledgements

Grateful acknowledgemnt is made to
the editors of the publications in which some of these poems or
versions of the poems first appeared:

Arsenic Lobster Poetry Journal, Bluestem,
CAIRN: The St. Andrews Review, Chiron Review,
Clackamas Literary Review, Coldnoon Travel Poetics,
Mochila Review, Sierra Nevada Review, Sour Grapes,
Textshop Experiments, Third Wednesday,
Tule Review, Welter: A Literary Journal

"For the Crows" also appeared as a letterpress broadside
with the same name (Baltimore: Hot Air Press, 2015)

Thanks

I am deeply grateful to many people
for their kindness and support of my work, especially
Josiah Bancroft, Felix Burgos, Landry Digeon, Phil Hartman,
Kendra Kopelke, Kenneth Pobo, Craig Saper, and Kitsi Watterson.

Special thanks to my family for their love and guidance, especially
my parents, Piotr Florczyk, and Molly LeGrand.

Finally, thanks to Bill Rutherford
and the collective that makes up Hot Air Press
for projecting this work into the world.

Biographical Note

K. A. Wisniewski is a Ph.D. Candidate in Language, Literacy & Culture at the University of Maryland Baltimore County (UMBC). He is the author of three artist books and is the editor of *The Comedy of Dave Chappelle: Critical Essays* (McFarland, 2009). His creative work has appeared in many journals, including *The Chariton Review, basalt, Toad Suck, Third Wednesday, The Chiron Review, MAYDAY Magazine, CAIRN,* and *The Sierra Nevada Review.* Wisniewski has held fellowships at the American Printing History Association, the Maryland Historical Society, and Boston College and has taught literature, history, and art at UMBC, Stevenson University, Widener University, the University of Baltimore, and Cecil College. He lives in Baltimore, Maryland.

HOT AIR PRESS

www.ingramcontent.com/pod-product-compliance
Lightning Source LLC
Chambersburg PA
CBHW071449040426
42445CB00012BA/1488